Come on a wild journey as you learn your NSW Foundation style cursive handwriting.

My name is

My school is

Learning goal: *To improve knowledge of the alphabet in NSW Foundation style handwriting*

Success criteria:

- *I can trace and write all lower-case letters of the alphabet in NSW Foundation style using both printing and cursive.*
- *I can trace and write all capital letters of the alphabet in NSW Foundation style.*

Are you ready to write?

Posture

Is your back resting against the chair?

Are your feet flat on the floor?

Paper position

left-handed

Are you holding the paper steady with your non-writing hand?

right-handed

Pencil grip

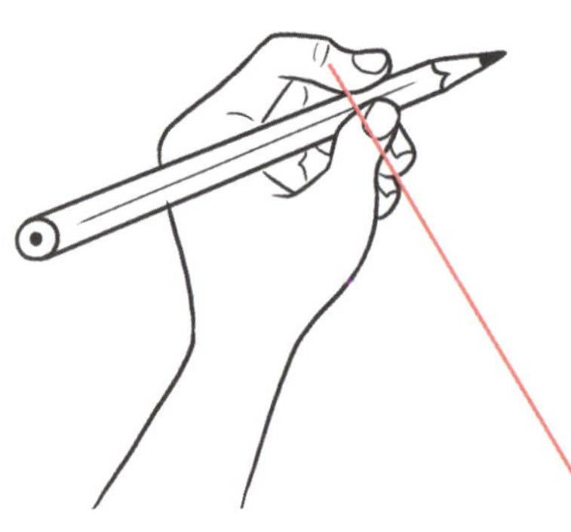

Is there only one finger on top of the pencil?

Left-handers, hold your pencil a little higher so you can see your handwriting!

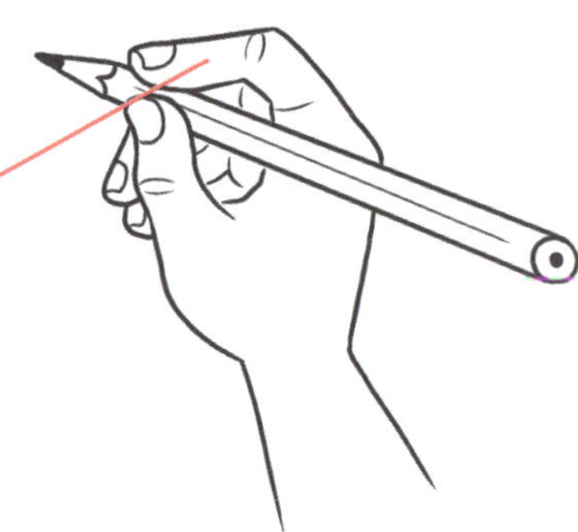

1, 2, 3, 4! Are my feet flat on the floor?
5, 6, 7, 8! Is my back up nice and straight?
9, 10, 11, 12! Show me how your pencil's held!
Thumb and pointer side-by-side, lucky tall one takes a ride!

Revising Foundation printing

Revise your Foundation printing.

aA bB cC dD eE fF gG

hH iI jJ kK lL mM nN

oO pP qQ rR sS tT uU

vV wW xX yY zZ

Copy the text.

This is NSW Foundation Style

printing. Most letters have a wedge.

Write the letters belonging to each group. The starting dots will give you clues. Write the letters in the order they appear in the alphabet.

Anti-clockwise movement (12)

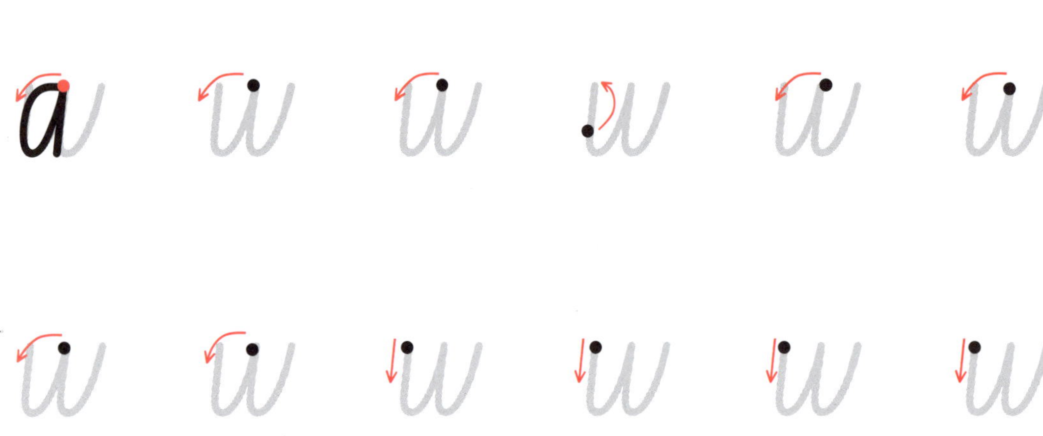

Clockwise movement (7)

Downstroke movement (7)

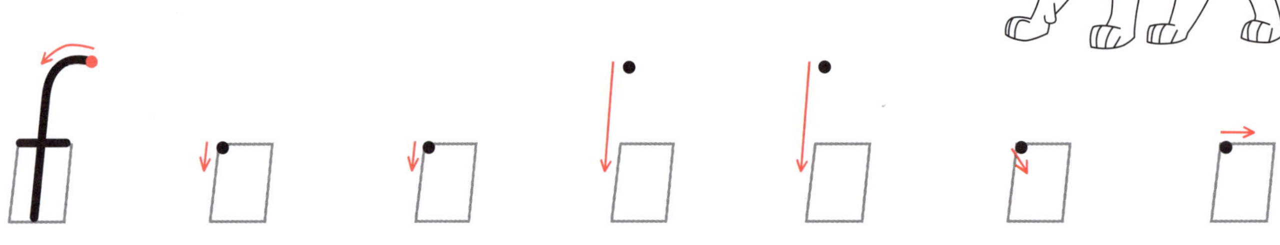

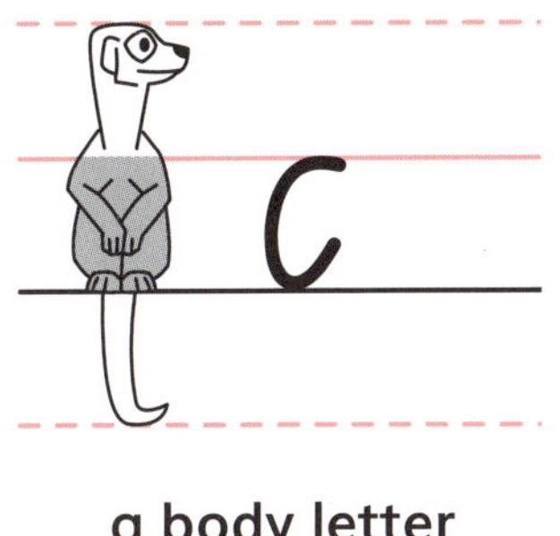

a body letter

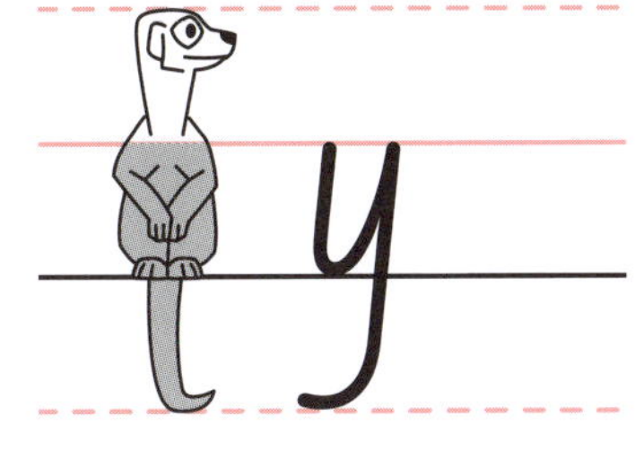

a body and tail letter

a head and body letter

Colour the parts of the meerkat to show what type of letter it is, then practise the letter.

Can you group the lower-case letters of the alphabet?

Body letters (14)

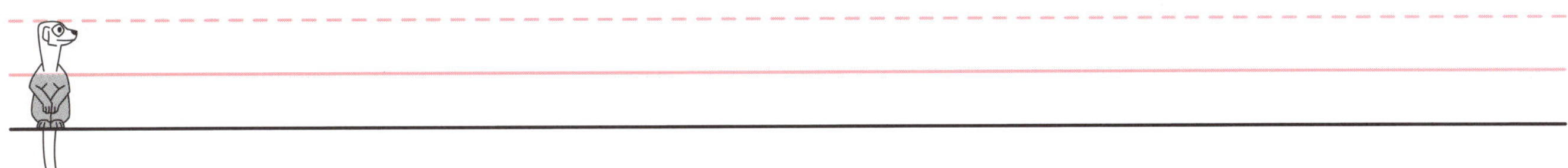

Head and body letters (7)

Body and tail letters (5)

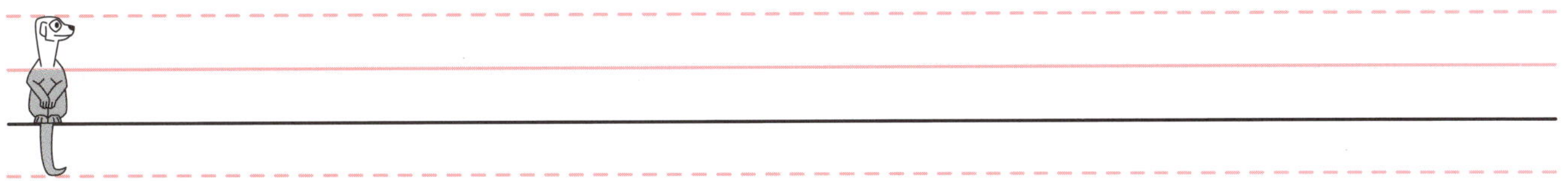

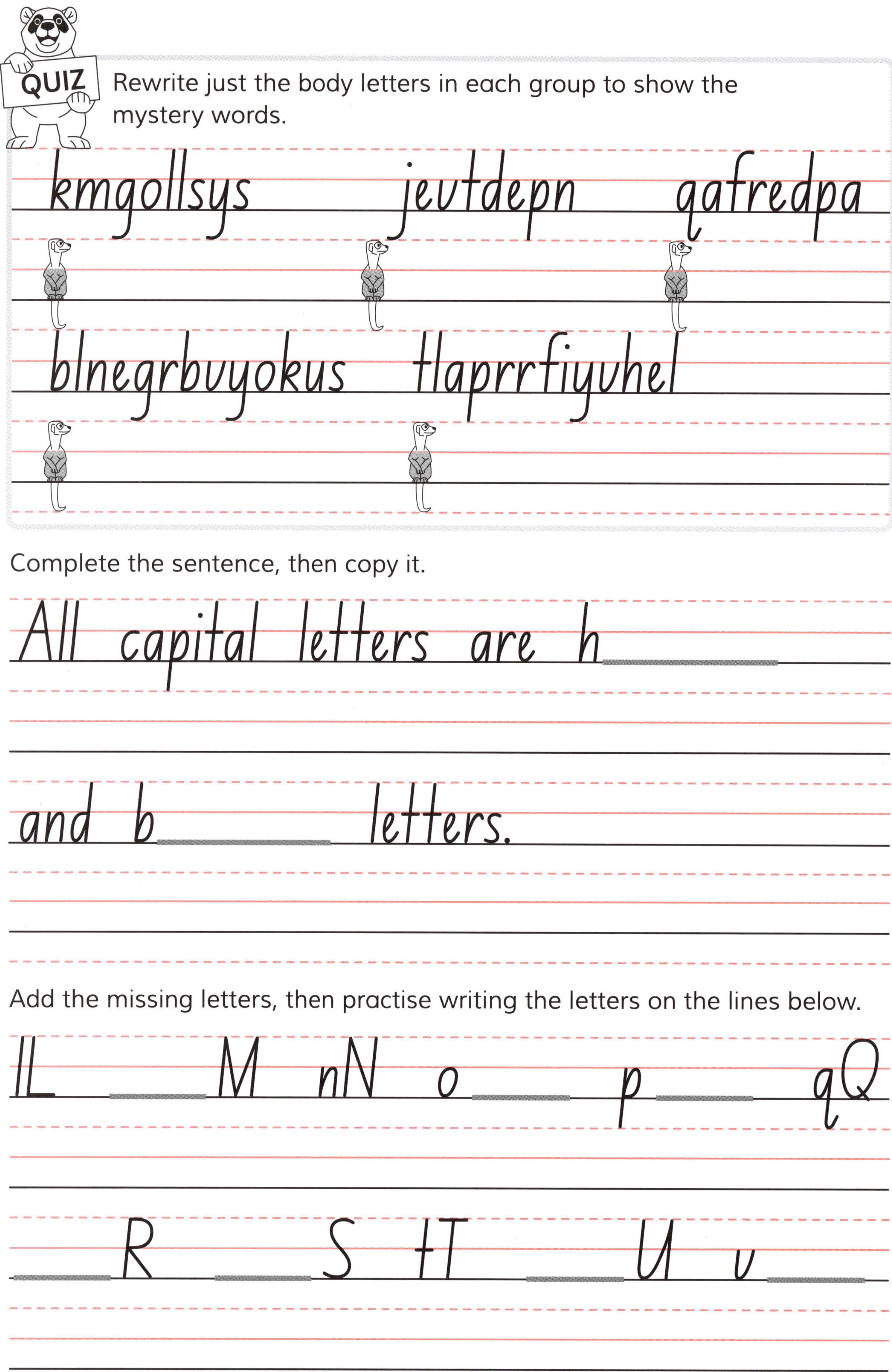

QUIZ Rewrite just the body letters in each group to show the mystery words.

kmgollsys jeutdepn qafredpa

blnegrbuyokus tlaprrfiyuhel

Complete the sentence, then copy it.

All capital letters are h_____

and b_____ letters.

Add the missing letters, then practise writing the letters on the lines below.

lL ____ M nN o____ p____ qQ

____R ____ S tT ____ U v____

Write these words in all capital letters.

Lower-case letters	Capital letters
australia	
antarctica	
europe	
africa	
asia	
north america	
south america	

Circle the words that should start with a capital letter.
Write only those words on the lines below.

april few monday city sydney most

harry english crept i'm elephant giggle

Trace and copy these patterns using all three movement groups.

Copy each numeral and bird name.

1. ostrich 2. emu 3. rhea 4. kiwi

Choose a location to match each bird.

New Zealand South America Australia South Africa

1. S Af

2.

3. S Am

4.

Copy the text.

Bar-tailed Godwits migrate from

Alaska to New Zealand every year.

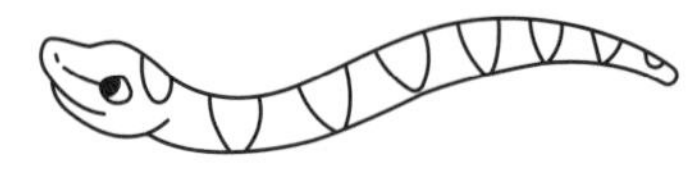

Draw a red dot to show the starting point of each letter, then practise the letter. Complete the lines.

d o
f x
b e
h a
p w

Colour all the wedges in the sentence.

Monarch Butterflies migrate to warmer places in winter.

get.ga/PMWA80

Self-assessment: Foundation printing

Copy the text.

Colour is important to butterflies.

It helps them to hide from their

enemies and to absorb heat. The

patterns on a butterfly's wings

are symmetrical.

Self-assessment

Rate your Foundation printing.

I need more practice.

It's fairly good.

It looks great!

Exits and entries

Introducing exits

An exit flick is a way out of a letter. It helps you join to the next letter.

a → a

Track these letters with exits.

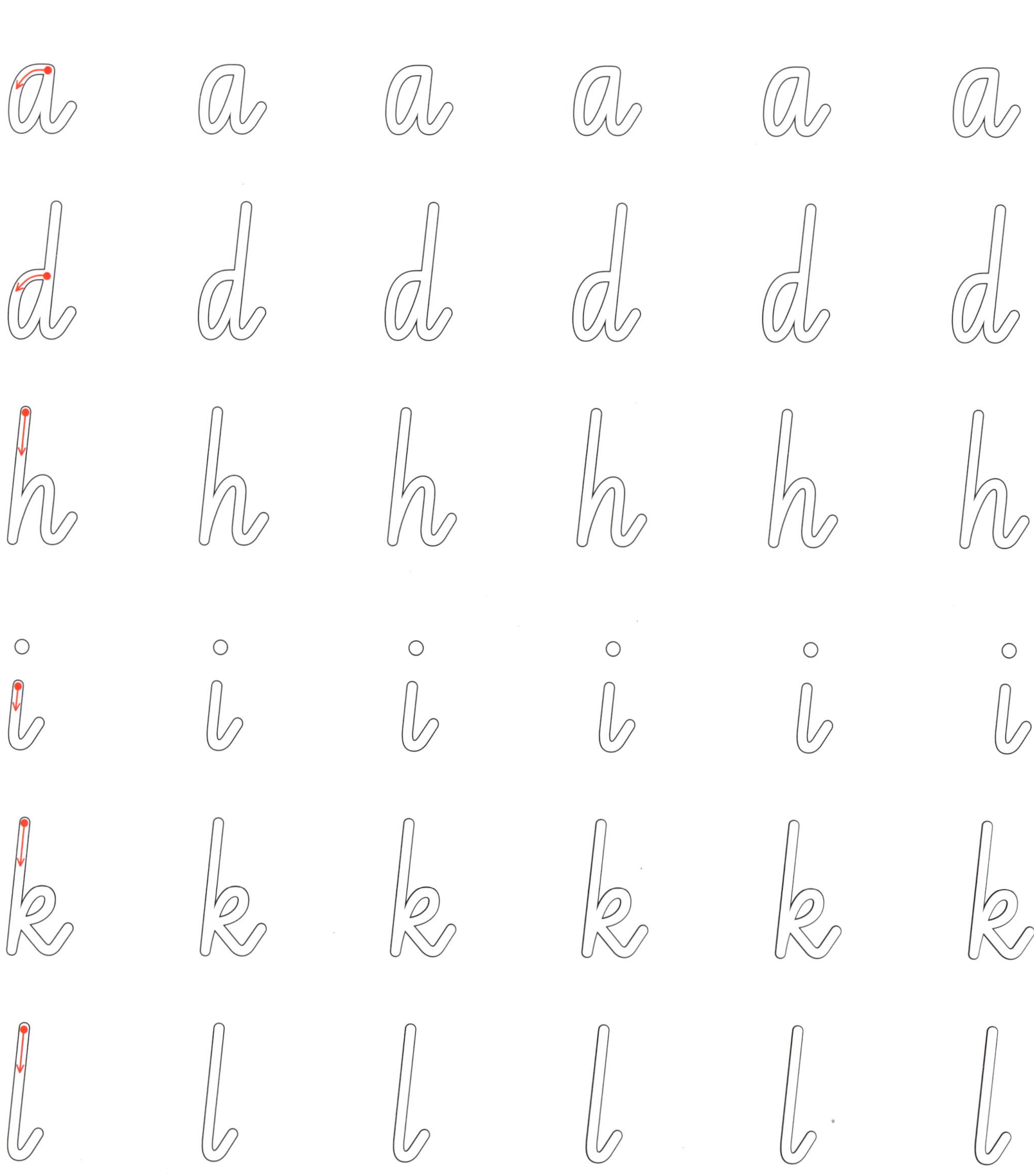

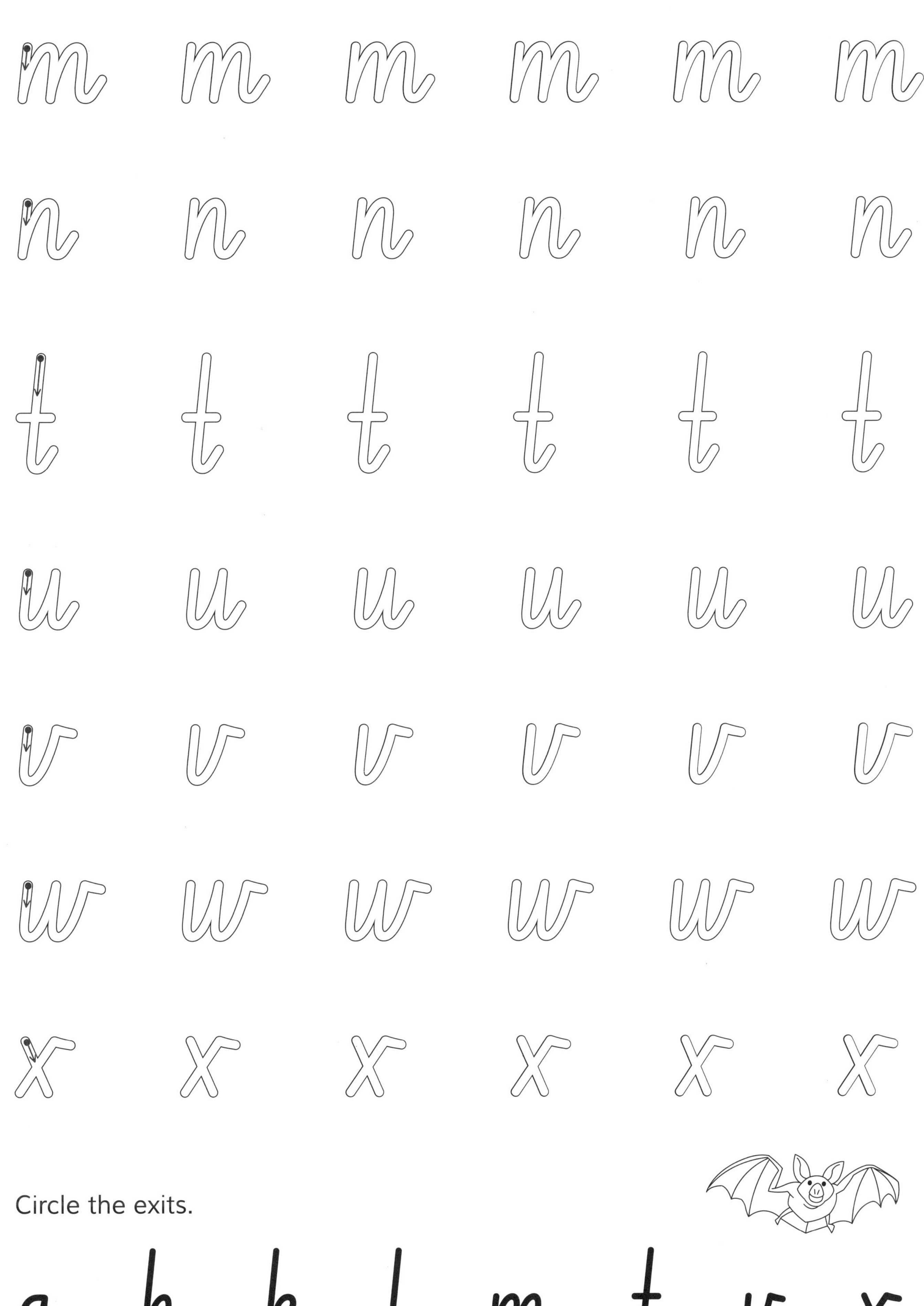

Circle the exits.

a h k l m t v x

Exit letters

Complete the line, then trace and copy.

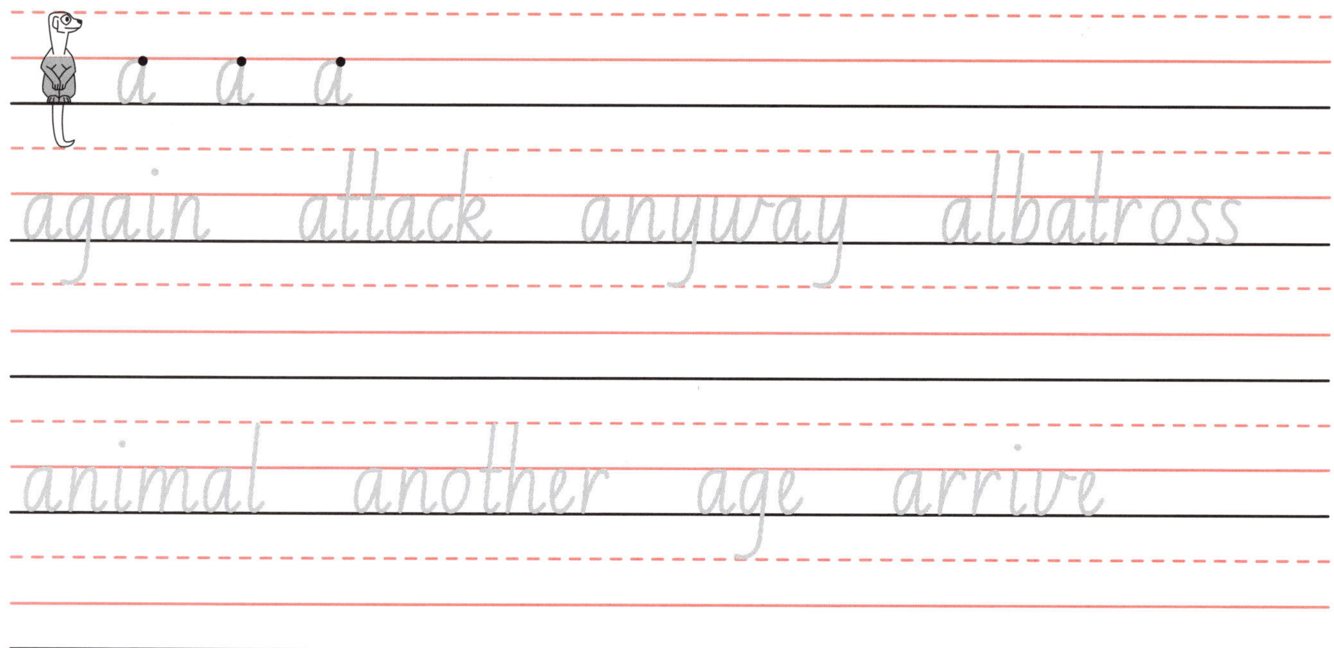

Complete the line, then trace and copy.

Complete the line, then trace and copy.

h h h

hawk hear shark half

hungry happen hyena heron

Complete the line, then trace and copy.

i i i

idea important indeed squid

isn't ice insect into iceberg

get.ga/PMWA81

My exit letters: a d h i k l m n t u v w x

Complete the line, then trace and copy.

k k k

knock kingfisher knee kill

kept kindly knew key

Complete the line, then trace and copy.

l l l

leap liked lion later lemur

lizard last learned llama

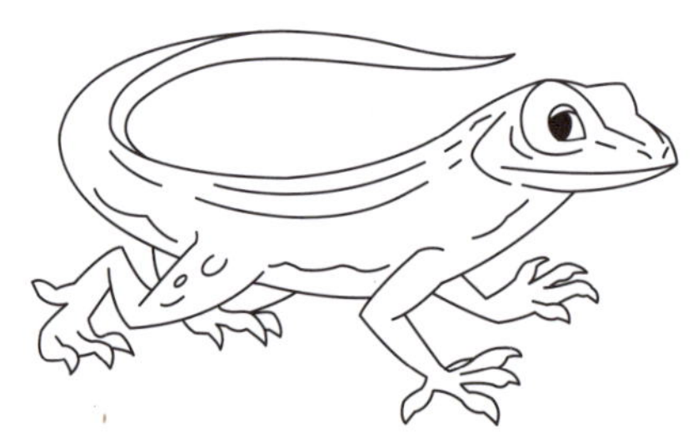

Complete the line, then trace and copy.

m m m

middle monkey camel moose

more moth moment meerkat

Complete the line, then trace and copy.

n n n

nothing nibbled noise near

nose nest numbat not

My exit letters: a d h i k l m n t u v w x

Complete the line, then trace and copy.

t t t

tallest teeth turtle toucan

torch tiger thick two

Complete the line, then trace and copy.

u u u

under uniform unpack

unlock underneath underwater

get.ga/PMWA82

Complete the line, then trace and copy.

v v v

volcano village voice over

valley vase raven never

Complete the line, then trace and copy.

w w w

wombat weather wonder

waiting walking warthog

My exit letters: a d h i k l m n t u v w x

Complete the line, then trace and copy.

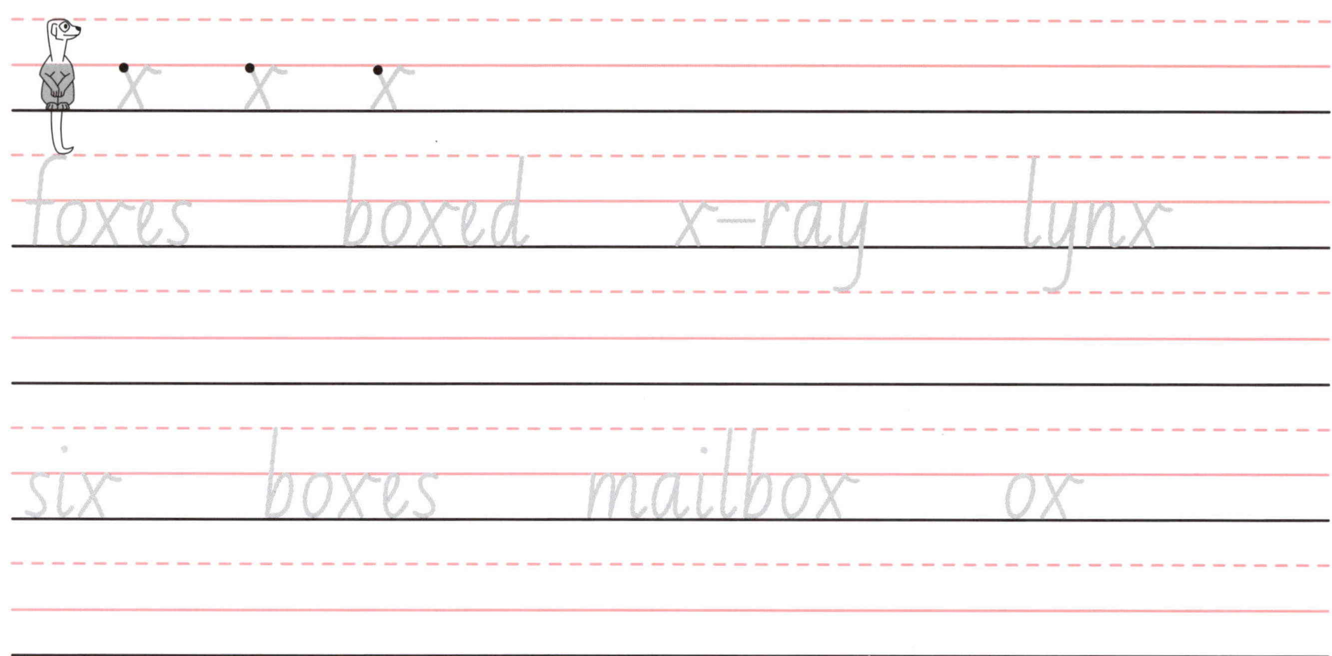

Copy each word. Use the exit letters you have learnt.

parrot jellyfish caribou bat

crocodile seal turtle lizard

Self-assessment: Exits

Copy the text.

A rainforest is a place of warmth
and high rainfall. It provides a
safe home for many living things.
Animals such as monkeys, frogs
and birds live among the plants.

Self-assessment

Rate your exit letters.

I need more practice.

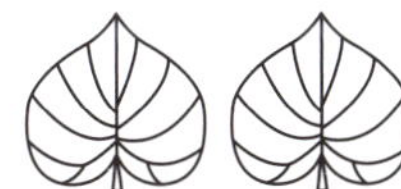

Good.

Great!

Introducing entries

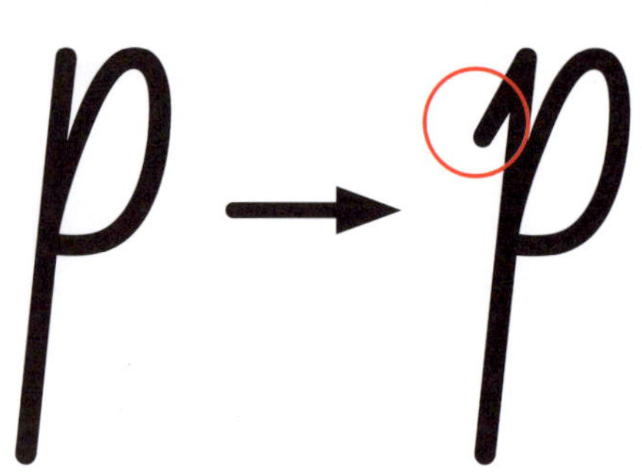

Track the entry letters.

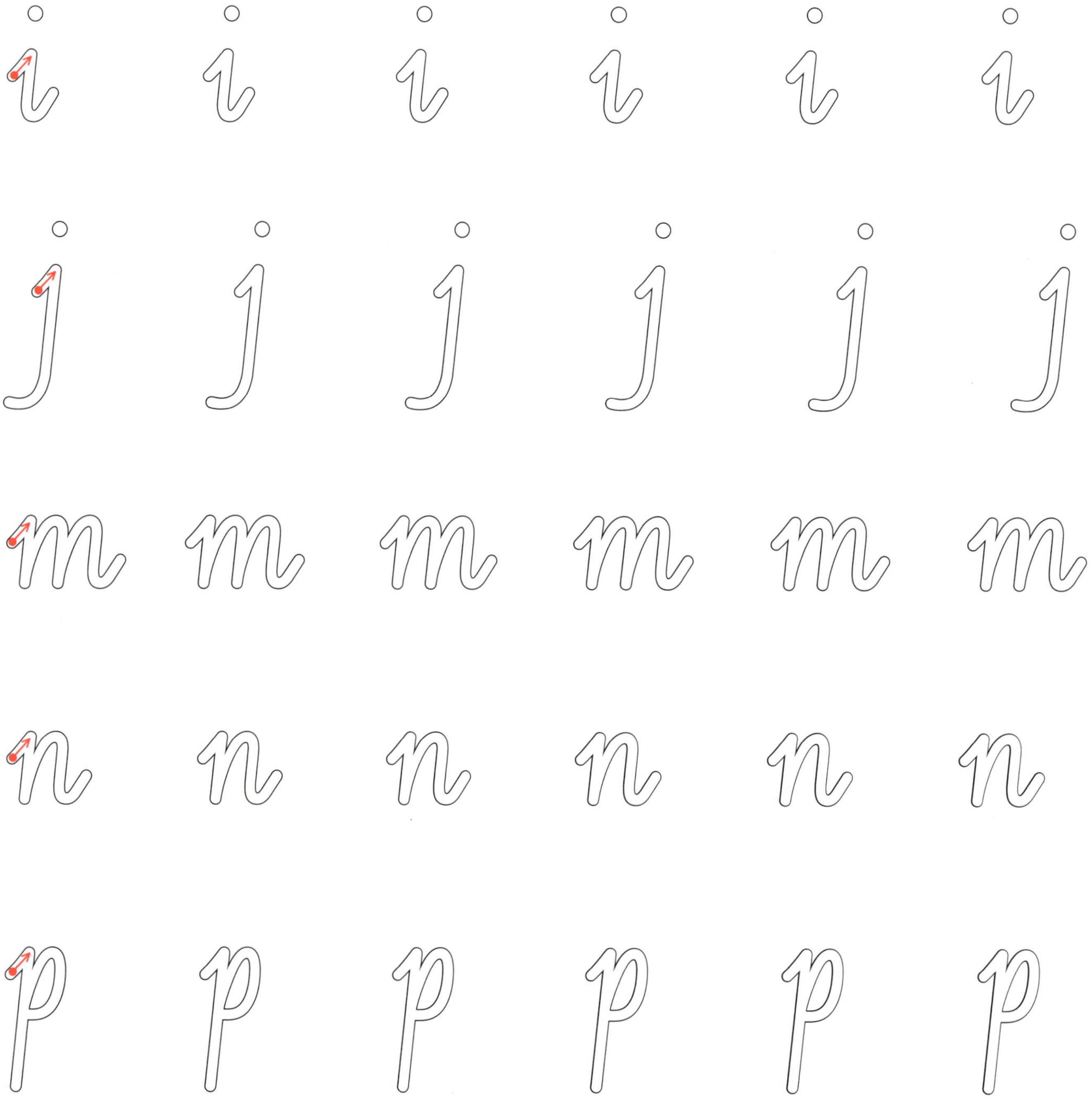

i i i i i i

j j j j j j

m m m m m m

n n n n n n

p p p p p p

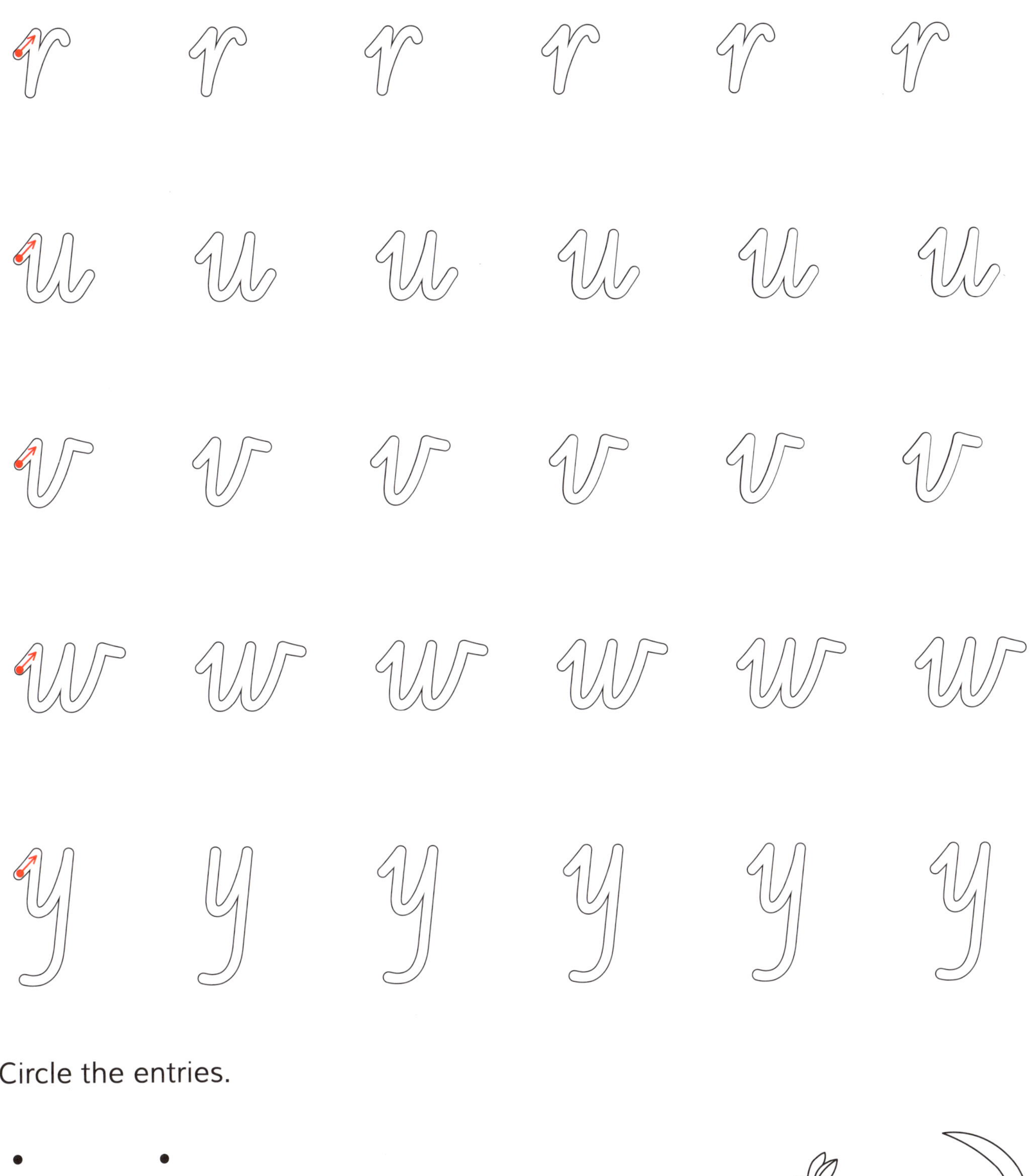

Circle the entries.

i j m n p

r u v w y

Entry letters

Complete the line, then trace and copy.

i i i

inside invitation ibis kingfisher

iguana island ice cream iron

Complete the line, then trace and copy.

j j j

jaws just jungle joins

jumped jacket jaguar jackal

Complete the line, then trace and copy.

m m m

myself moonlight move

mountain mouse meadow

Complete the line, then trace and copy.

n n n

notice nowhere never

numbat narwhal nest

Complete the line, then trace and copy.

p p p

pushed panda power parrot

past people penguins part

Complete the line, then trace and copy.

r r r

ready reach rhinoceros

rumbled roared raccoon

Complete the line, then trace and copy.

u u u

understand undo undergrowth

until uniform upstairs

Complete the line, then trace and copy.

v v v

vest vinegar vowel viper

vulture village voice valley

Complete the line, then trace and copy.

w w w

would world whale water

wombat whistle wetlands

Complete the line, then trace and copy.

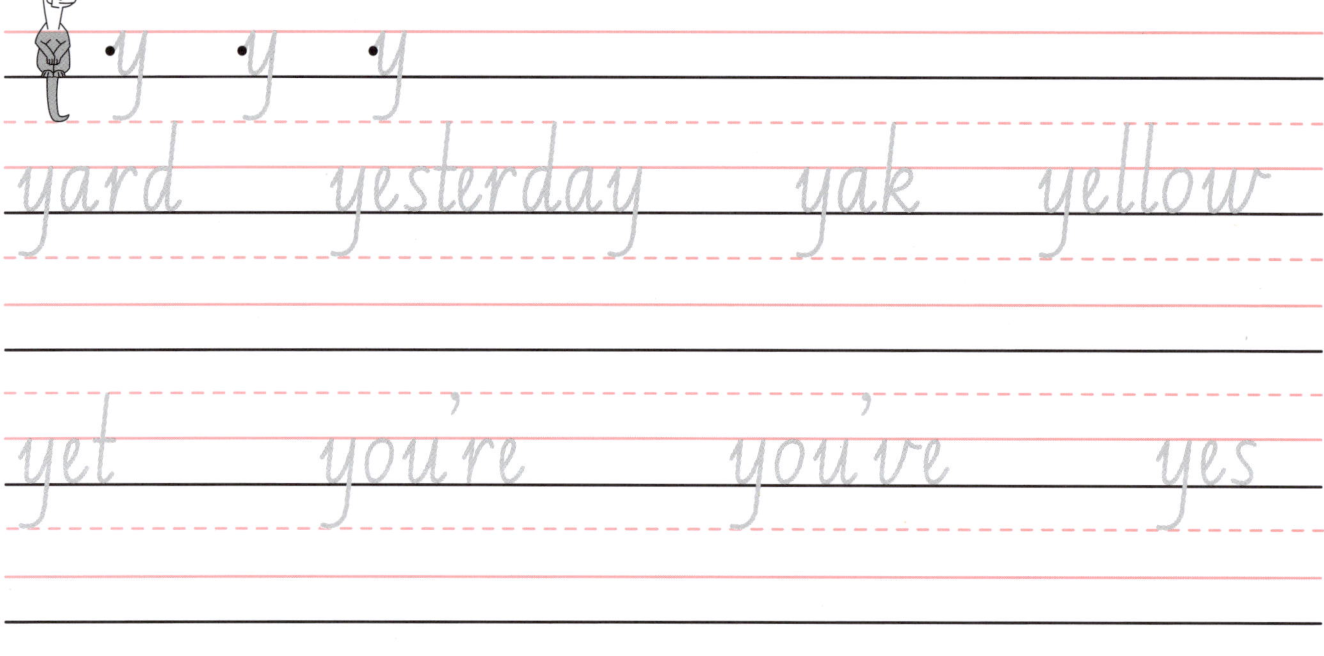

Self-assessment: Entries

Copy the text.

Hyenas are wild animals that like to laugh.

Q: Why do bears have fur coats?

A: Because they would look silly wearing a jacket!

Self-assessment

Rate your entry letters.

I need to keep practising.

They've improved.

They look good!

Letters with exits and entries

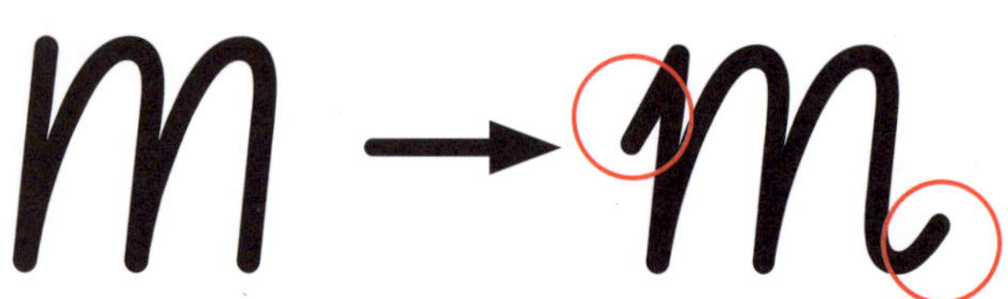

Circle the exits and entries.

i m n u v w

Complete the line, then trace and copy.

How many exits and entries in this word?

camouflage

Self-assessment: Letters with exits and entries

Rewrite these sentences, adding entries and exits to the letters that need them.

Jellyfish live in ocean currents.

A large group is called a smack.

A jellyfish's body is mostly filled

with water. Long tentacles hang

from the edge of a jellyfish's body.

Self-assessment

Rate your entries and exits.

☐ I need to keep practising.

☐ They've improved.

☐ They look good!

Introducing joins

tallest exits and entries

tallest cursive

Copy the text with exits and entries.

Join lines join one letter to

the next letter.

In cursive, most letters are joined.

Trace and copy these patterns to practise join lines.

acaca hihi mnmn

elel twtwt awawa

Diagonal joins

ai → ai

Trace and copy these letter pairs with diagonal joins.

ai ap au av aw ay ai ap

ci cu cy di du dy ci cu cy

ei ep eu ew ey hi hu ei ep

iw ki ky li lp lu iw ki ky

ly mi mp mu my ni ti ly

Trace and copy these letter pairs with diagonal joins.

am an ar cr dr em en

er ex im in ir mm mn

nn tr um un ur ux le

ne ae ee te he ce ie de

Trace and copy these words using diagonal joins.

air jaw monkey tip stingray

Copy the alphabet with diagonal joins.

abcdefghijklmnopqrstuvwxyz

Copy these words with diagonal joins.

time her like cheetah

then they them tell link

quite purring marlin fur

bee pile nine little mammal

Diagonal joins to head and body letters

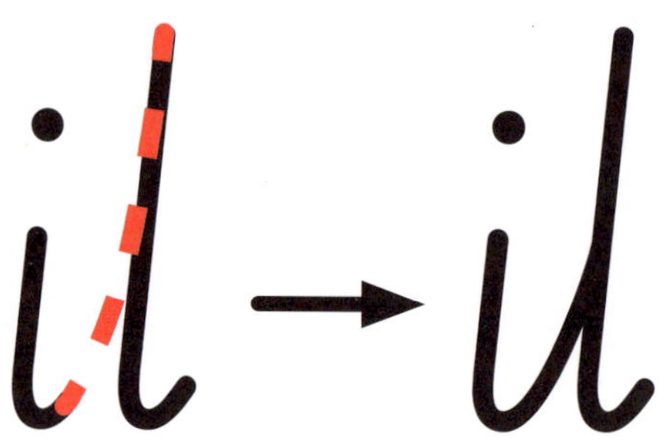

When joining to head and body letters, sweep up to the top and down again.

Trace and copy these letter pairs with diagonal joins to head and body letters.

mb nt th tt ub ul ut

Choose a letter pair from above to make a word on each line below.

b________ fa________ h________

l________ pa________ n________

co________ gr________ ro________

Copy these words with diagonal joins to head and body letters.

about invitation chameleon

spill buckle almost channel

lantern anteater patter nestle

Make these verbs past tense by adding –ed, then complete the line.

float + ed →

call + ed →

Here is a wild animal joke for you.

Copy the text.

Q: What's the world's biggest ant?

A: An eleph–ant.

Complete the line, practising the diagonal join.

ly ly

Rewrite the word, using any diagonal joins and adding -ly.

careful + ly → carefully

quiet + ly →

quick + ly →

loud + ly →

soft + ly →

Complete the line, practising the diagonal join.

er er

Rewrite the word, using any diagonal joins and adding -er.

long + er →

strong + er →

loud + er →

fast + er →

Add -ly or -er to these words. Be careful your new words are spelt correctly.

bright →

deep →

green →

lean →

own →

part →

poor →

thick →

tall →

short →

brave →

swift →

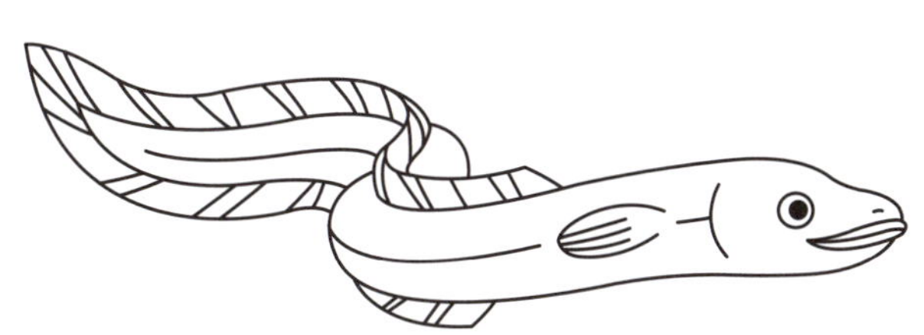

Diagonal joins from 'q'

q

A 'q' can be tricky — you need to quickly change direction and go all the way up to the top.

Don't be quarrelsome! The movement is the same every time — a 'q' is always followed by a 'u'.

Trace.

q q q q q q q

qu qu qu qu qu qu qu

Trace and copy.

A quokka looks like a small

kangaroo. Many live on Rottnest

Island. A quoll is nocturnal and

likes to sleep in hollow logs.

Diagonal joins from 'z'

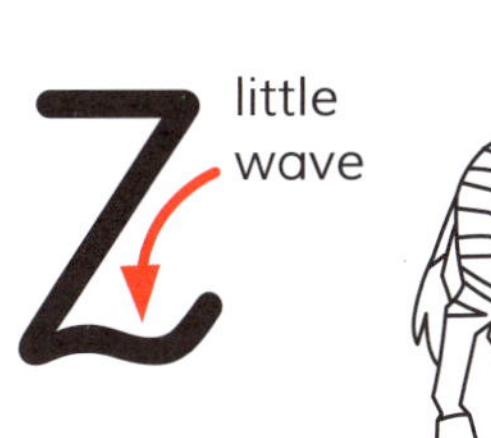

Don't get caught napping when you are joining from the letter 'z'. Make a little wave with your pencil before you do the diagonal join to the next letter.

Trace.

z z z z z z z

zi zl zy ze zi zl zy ze

Trace and copy.

When you visit a zoo, make

sure you zip along to the zebra

enclosure. Notice that every zebra

has different stripes. Amazing!

Self-assessment: Diagonal joins

Copy these letter pairs in cursive.

au ai ly mu ni hy ej ki lu mi

nu ty ui ai an cr em ir mm

Rewrite this joke in cursive. Use any diagonal join you know.

Q: What did the pony say

when it had a sore throat?

A: I'm a little hoarse.

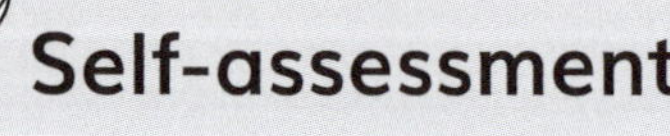

Self-assessment

Rate your diagonal joins.

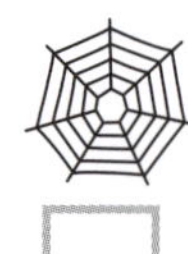

I need to work on them.

Getting there.

They look great!

Drop-in joins

The following letters use an anti-clockwise movement.

When you join diagonally to one of the letters above, make a longer exit from the letter before. Then, lift your pencil and drop the second letter into place.

Copy these letters with long exits.

n m i e a d

h k t l c u

Diagonal joins to the anti-clockwise letters are called drop-in joins.

Use two colours to trace the drop-in joins. Make the exit of the first letter longer, and drop in the second letter. The arrows show the pencil lifts.

Try some more letter pairs using two colours.

n na nc nd ng no na

a ac ad ag ao aq ac

d da dd do da dd do

i ia ic id ig ia ic iq

e ea ec ed eg eo eq ea

get.ga/PMWA84

Draw an arrow to show the drop-in joins.

animal predator scales

attack habitat mammal

claws sloth tail aquatic

Practise your drop-in joins. Copy the text.

The echidna is a mammal that lays eggs. When an egg hatches, a hairless baby, or puggle, is born. A puggle is the size of a jelly bean.

Create a name for this puggle using as many drop-in joins as possible.

Count the number of drop-in joins the words below would have in cursive. Prove your answers by writing the words.

underneath ☐ gliding ☐ puggle ☐

Write these words with drop-in joins. Underline every drop-in join.

echidna guard python edge

liquid paddle suddenly change

magnificent meadow aground

dance wetlands underground

Try rainbow writing. Copy each word, changing colour every time you make a drop-in join.

feathers

covered

chick

puggle

underwater

cockatoo

Antarctica

jaguar

aquarium

peacock

catching

toucan

Drop-in joins to 'f'

f → f

'f' is now a head, body and tail letter.

Complete the line, then trace and copy.

f f f

off fork rainforest buffalo

flightless frog flocks few fly

crossbar and exit flick

af

When dropping in 'f', extend the exit flick of the letter before it, then start 'f' at the top. Make sure the crossbar meets the exit flick.

Trace and copy.

if af uf if mf nf lf ef

life safety wolf horrified after

Self-assessment: Drop-in joins

Copy the text.

Blue whales have no teeth.

A baby swan is called a cygnet.

A group of bats is called a colony.

Butterflies can taste with their feet.

A baby dolphin is a calf.

Self-assessment

Rate your drop-in joins.

☐ I need more practice.

☐ They're good.

☐ I'm very confident!

Horizontal joins

The letters that finish near the top body line form horizontal joins.

o r v w x

✓ on ✗ on

When making a horizontal join, don't dip the join too low.

Trace and copy.

or rn rr vy rp wi wm oy

ou vu rr ry vi vv on om

pony vulture squirrel

horse forest monkey

Trace and copy.

or wr ow ov ru oi un wu

op ow on rr oz rm ri rv

wren cow dove hopping lion

xi xi

With 'x' you have a choice. It can join to the next letter with a horizontal line or it can stay unjoined.

Trace and copy with 'x' unjoined.

xp xy xu xi xp xy xu xi

Trace and copy with 'x' joined to the next letter.

xp xy xu xi xp xy xu xi

Horizontal joins to anti-clockwise letters

When making a horizontal join to an anti-clockwise letter, a little retracing is required.

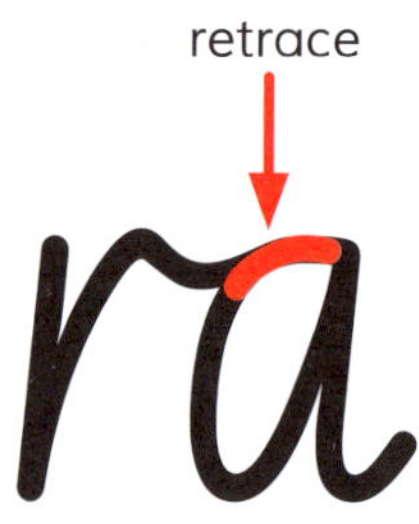

oc

Trace and copy.

oo oa od og ra va oo oa od

crawl zoo codfish dog coat

rd wa ra oc rc rd wa ra oc

herd octopus wander scramble

Trace and copy.

ra wa vo ro va ra wa xa xo

extra vole crouch hexagon

wa ro rd rg wo wa ro rd rg

wrong heard crown walk birds

Give each word below an antonym (word of opposite meaning) from the word bank. Use any joins you already know.

backwards —

broad —

wavy —

awkward —

cool —

narrow
warm
straight
graceful
forwards

Horizontal joins to head and body letters

When making a horizontal join to a head and body letter, sweep up and down, retracing a little.

Trace and copy these letter pairs with horizontal joins to head and body letters.

ob oh ok ol ot rb rh

rl rt wh wl wt wb xt

wf xf of rf wf of rf xf

Trace and copy.

rhinoceros warthog hollow

okay waterhole growl tortoise

Trace and copy.

Thirteen rhinos came to the

waterhole where they felt safe.

Fourteen warthogs joined their

party. Fortunately, they heard

the growl of a nearby lion and

escaped. They were all okay.

Reread the text. How many animals in total at the waterhole?

Horizontal joins from 'f'

fu fi

When joining letters from 'f', use the crossbar to make a straight horizontal line to the next letter.

Trace.

fu fi fu fi fu fi fu fi fu

fur fish fungi fist fight furry

fe fl

'f' doesn't join to 'e'. When 'f' joins to 'l', retrace the downstroke of the 'l'.

Trace.

fe fl fe fl fe fl fe fl

flight feed flounder feet fear flick

fa fo

Remember to retrace when joining 'f' to 'a' or 'o'.

Trace.

fa fo fa fo fa fo fa fo

forests food family fossil faster

Self-assessment: Horizontal joins

Copy the text.

A herd of fifty caribou moved
from the frozen north. In the
south, they sought shelter in the
forests of fir trees. They worked
together to keep their babies safe.

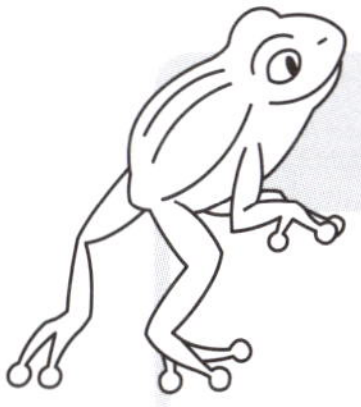

Self-assessment

Rate your horizontal joins.

I need more practice. They're getting there. They're great!

get.ga/PMWA85

Letters that do not join

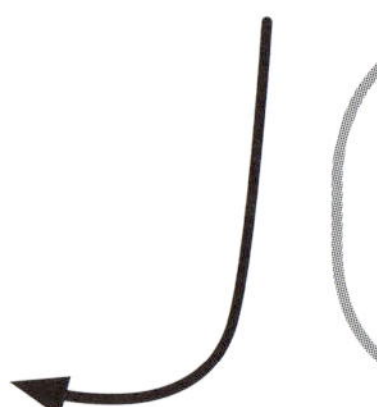

Letters that finish in a clockwise direction do not join to the next letter.

Trace and copy these clockwise finishers.

b g j p s y

Complete the sentence below with the correct word or words from the word bank, using cursive. Then copy the sentence.

exit	flick	entry

Letters that do not join to the next letter have no ____________.

Capital letters don't join to other letters.

Trace the animal names and then write the country they live in, using cursive.

Australia Greenland India
Brazil South Africa China

reindeer

meerkat

tiger

wombat

boa constrictor

panda

fe oe re ve we xe

Letters that finish near the top body line do not join to 'e'.

Copy the text.

get.ga/PMWA86

web different even live rear doe

covered prey spread tree very

feather axe feet executive feed boxes

Some spiders spin sticky webs.

They use their delicate feet to

wrap their prey in silk threads.

Self-assessment: Letters that do not join

Rewrite the following text in cursive, adding capital letters where needed.

there are many amazing wild animals on our planet. sadly, humans don't always treat animals well. the good news is that we can help save them.

Self-assessment

How well do you remember your letters that don't join?

I need more practice.

I'm getting there.

I always remember!

Numerals

Practise your times tables. Copy and complete.

5 × 3 = 15 2 × 7 = 14

10 × 11 = 110 5 × ____ = 40

2 × 6 = ____ 10 × 12 = ____

5 × 5 = 25 2 × ____ = 18

Copy the patterns on the wings of the butterflies. Be careful to make them symmetrical.

Create your own butterfly patterns. Can you copy each one carefully onto the matching wing?

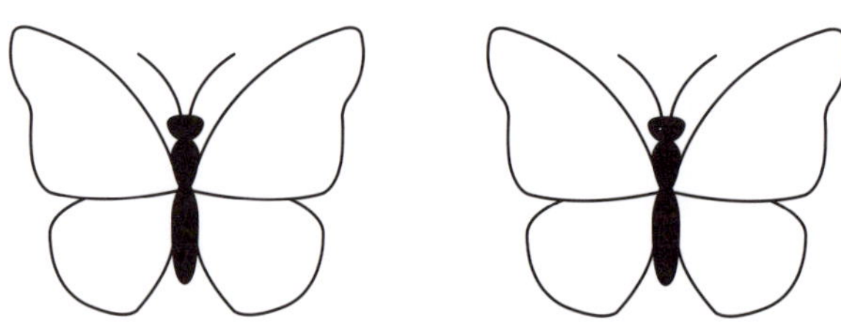

Final self-assessment

Copy the text, then complete the self-assessment below.

Polar Bears live near the North Pole. They use their great sense of smell to hunt seals. Seal oil can make their fur yellow. They use their claws to dig into the ice.

Self-assessment

Rate your NSW Foundation style cursive.

☐ It's getting there.

☐ Good.

☐ Excellent!

Teacher observation guide

Student is: left-handed ☐ right-handed ☐

Student demonstrates correct posture, paper position and pencil grip. ☐

Student forms the NSW Foundation style alphabet (lower-case and capital letters) with accuracy. ☐

Student uses head, body and tail character to describe the spatial properties of letters, and can group letters accordingly. ☐

Student understands the three basic movement groups to which letters belong (anti-clockwise, clockwise, downstroke). ☐

Student can trace and copy patterns using all three movements with accuracy. ☐

Student can identify and colour wedges. ☐

Student can accurately write letters with exits and entries. ☐

Student forms diagonal joins with accuracy. ☐

Student forms drop-in joins with accuracy. ☐

Student forms horizontal joins with accuracy. ☐

Student can identify the letters that do not join in the NSW Foundation style. ☐

Student can join to and from the letter 'f' with accuracy. ☐

Student can join from the letters 'q' and 'z' with accuracy. ☐

Student can convert between scripts: print, cursive and capital letters. ☐

Student can copy a complete passage of text with accuracy using cursive script in the NSW Foundation style. ☐

Student can self-assess with accuracy. ☐

Notes:

....

....

Date:

....

CERTIFICATE

get.ga/PMWC80